Joseph

Words by Anna Fienberg • Pictures by Kim Gamble

ALLEN & UNWIN

Listen now, and I'll tell you the story of Joseph. You would have loved him – his quick smile, his shining eyes, his telling of dreams.

He could tell you the future!

You see, Joseph was born with a special gift. He understood the meaning of dreams. If you came to him and whispered yours, he'd turn to you with that quick smile of his and reveal the deepest secrets of your life.

Jacob, Joseph's father, loved him with all his heart. Jacob had eleven other sons, too, and that's counting the new baby, Benjamin. But you could see that when Joseph brought him his supper or handed him his wine, Jacob's face lit up like the sun.

It wasn't easy being a brother of Joseph, the dreamer.

'Why does *Joseph* get all the praise?' said Simeon.

'Why does he get the most tender piece of lamb?' raged Dan.

'It isn't fair,' said Levi, thumping the ground.

One morning Joseph woke up early and shook his brothers awake. 'I've had an amazing dream!' he whispered. 'Listen!' His eyes were blazing with the memory of it. 'We were binding sheaves of corn out in the field when suddenly my sheaf rose and stood upright, while your sheaves gathered round mine and bowed down to it.'

The brothers scowled. 'So you think you're going to rule over us like a king, do you?' sneered Simeon.

But the next morning Joseph had another dream, and he couldn't help but tell it. That was the trouble with Joseph. The dream-world inside his mind swirled like a rainbow sea, rolling in, rolling back, leaving treasures on the shore. How could he *not* share them?

'This time,' said Joseph, 'I dreamed that the sun and moon and eleven stars were bowing down to me.'

Even Jacob was annoyed. 'What does this mean?' he cried. 'Are you telling me that your mother and I and all your brothers will actually bow down to the ground before you?'

But it was a dream that Joseph, and his father, would never forget.

Joseph was blessed. He could read dreams as easily as cloud patterns will tell a storm. He had a special gift. But sometimes a gift is so big that it makes a shadow. And for many years Joseph had to live inside the shadow of his gift, instead of the light.

Joseph and his brothers went on tending their father's sheep each day in the hot dusty fields of Canaan. Every morning they'd set out early as the sun rose, and return at sunset. As they watched Joseph, the hatred inside Joseph's brothers grew. The more he shone, with his stories and his smiles and his dreamy eyes, the duller and more gloomy they felt. Like old stones blackening round a fire. And when, one evening, Jacob gave Joseph a present of a splendid coat, glowing with all the colours of the rainbow, the brothers exploded.

'And where are *our* coats?' they cried to each other. 'Does Jacob think he has only one son?'

It was then that they decided to kill Joseph.

The brothers were already in the fields with the sheep when Joseph came panting towards them. He'd been chatting with his father, and as he ran the coat flew out behind him, red and gold and indigo, like the royal robe of the heavens.

'Here comes that dreamer!' one of the brothers hissed. 'Come on, let's kill him and throw him into one of these wells.'

'We'll say that a ferocious animal devoured him,' said another. 'Then we'll see what comes of his dreams.'

But one of the brothers loved Joseph better.

'Let's not take his life,' said Reuben. 'See that old well over there? Dry as a bone. Throw him into it. But don't shed any blood.'

And I'll come back in the evening and rescue him, thought Reuben.

Quickly the brothers stripped young Joseph of his magnificent coat, and threw him into the well. His cries were strangled by the thick earth walls of his prison.

During the morning a sheep wandered off, and Reuben hurried away to find it. He was still away at midday, when the brothers sat down in the field to eat their lunch. (How could they *swallow* it, do you think?) As they passed around a flask of wine, they saw a caravan of merchants and camels loping along the horizon. The camels were loaded up with spices, balm and myrrh, bound for Egypt.

'That's it!' cried Judah, slapping his knee. 'Why don't we sell our little Joseph to those merchants? Then he'll be so far away we won't even have to think of him – and there'll be no blood on our hands!'

Reuben was not there to see the look of relief and cunning that sharpened his brothers' faces.

So that is how it happened. The brothers sold Joseph for twenty shekels of silver to the merchants, who took him far away from his homeland, to Egypt.

But now what would the brothers tell Jacob, the most loving of fathers? The truth? *Never*. They took a goat and cut its throat and drowned Joseph's coat with its blood. Then they trudged home to their father, their legs heavy with guilt. When Jacob saw his sons, their faces dark as the falling dusk, he felt a tremor in his heart.

'Where is Joseph?' he cried.

Silently Simeon handed him the bloodied rainbow coat.

Jacob put the coat to his cheek. He stroked the rich material, stiff with blood. 'This is my son's robe,' he whispered. 'Some fearsome animal has torn my child to pieces.'

The brothers tried to comfort him, but he pushed them away. He tore at his clothes and his hair, and wept for days and weeks. He was like a river flooding its banks, fed by an ocean of sorrow.

But do you suppose that a bit of distance – a few hundred kilometres – could make the brothers forget what they'd done? Do you imagine that this was the end of Joseph?

'Didn't I tell you not to sin against the boy?' Reuben cried every night. 'You wouldn't listen! You'll see, something dreadful will happen to us, it will, it will!' But the other brothers wanted to hear none of it, and they slouched away, muttering nothings to blot out the echo of Reuben's words.

Now at that time, the Pharaoh-King ruled over all Egypt. He and his guards were rich and powerful (*so* rich it'd take your breath away), and they brought people from other countries to make their bricks and tend their fields and build their houses. These people became slaves of the Egyptians, and they were ordered about and sold like animals.

And that is what happened to our Joseph.

A man called Potiphar, captain of Pharaoh's guard, bought Joseph as his slave. He took him to his finely decorated home, and watched him as he worked.

As the weeks passed, Potiphar saw that Joseph was different. He seemed blessed, somehow. Everything he did, he did well. With the other servants he was kind and helpful. He organised his work and theirs, always speaking with that quick smile of his, always ready to offer help.

Potiphar was so pleased with Joseph that he put him in charge of the entire household. 'Everything I own,' Potiphar told Joseph, 'is in your care. I'd trust you with my life.'

But somebody else in that fine home was watching Joseph, too. Potiphar's wife had noticed Joseph's warm smile and shining eyes. She'd noticed his strong shoulders and smooth broad chest – and what about that easy, close way he joked with the others and told them his dreams? She wanted to be close to him, too. Very close.

One morning, when Potiphar was away, she grabbed Joseph's hands and tried to kiss him. But Joseph pushed her away.

'No,' he said. 'How could I betray your husband this way? He has trusted me with everything he owns. I'd never hurt him.'

Potiphar's wife pleaded with Joseph, each day begging and insisting, but still Joseph refused her. Then one day she grew so angry, she shouted out to the guards, 'Arrest this man – he came in here to steal me away! He tried to kiss me!'

When Potiphar heard this tale, he burned with rage. Calling his guards, he cried, 'Take this slave to the dungeons so that I may never see his face again!'

The days crawled by, and the fire of Potiphar's rage died away. Only a hard lump of sorrow smouldered in his chest. Potiphar missed Joseph, and the easy way he ran the house. But how could he ever forgive him?

Meanwhile, Joseph worked busily in the dim, dark dungeons. He didn't despair. He seemed blessed, somehow. Everything he did, he did well. His warm smile and telling of dreams had made him special to the prison warder, and soon Joseph was put in charge of all the people in the dungeons.

Now it happened that two years after Joseph was arrested, the mighty Pharaoh began to have dreams. Strange, troubling dreams. He couldn't understand them but they haunted him like ghosts, even while he was awake. All the magicians and wise men of Egypt were sent for, but no one could explain what the dreams meant.

It was the Pharaoh's servants who helped solve the puzzle. A butler and cook had been sent to prison for a short time, and there they had met Joseph. They remembered that fine-looking man, the master of dreams. And Joseph was brought before the Pharaoh.

'The dream was so real, as real as this throne I am sitting on,' the Pharaoh began.

'Tell me,' said Joseph.

'Well, I was standing by the River Nile when out of the water came seven cows, all sleek and fat. They began grazing among the reeds. After them came seven more cows, all thin and scrawny. The cows were standing side by side on the riverbank, when suddenly, the thin, ugly cows gobbled up the fat ones! It was horrible.'

'Hmmm,' said Joseph thoughtfully.

'Then I fell asleep again,' the Pharaoh went on. 'And I had another dream. Seven ears of corn, healthy and golden, were growing on a single stalk. After them, seven other ears of corn sprouted – thin and scorched by the east wind. The thin ears of corn swallowed up the seven healthy ears. And then I woke up. What can it mean? Can you tell me?'

Joseph nodded. 'The two dreams you had mean the same thing. My God has shown you what he's about to do, and you must listen. The fat cows and healthy corn are his promise that you'll have seven years of plenty. The land will blossom and the harvests will be huge. The thin cows and blighted corn tell you that seven years of famine will follow.'

The Pharaoh looked hard at Joseph. He knew in his heart this was right, and that Joseph was blessed as a master of dreams. 'What do you advise me to do then?'

'Choose a man and put him in charge of the land of Egypt. He should make sure all the extra food collected during the good times is stored for the harsh years that follow.'

The Pharaoh smiled. 'Since God has made all this clear to you, the choice is easy. I see no one else around who is as wise or as honourable as you.'

So our Joseph was made governor of the whole land of Egypt. The Pharaoh gave him his signet ring, dressed him in fine clothes and took him everywhere in his chariot. 'No one will lift hand or foot in all Egypt,' commanded Pharaoh, 'unless they have the word of Joseph.'

And it all happened just as Joseph had said. For seven years the fertile land overflowed with grain and Joseph organised the extra food to be stored in great silos in the cities. And then the River Nile dried up and the land became dust and the corn blackened in the fields.

During the famine the people of Egypt still had bread to eat, because Joseph had planned so well. But all the countries around Egypt were starving. They had feasted during the great harvests and now had nothing. So they had to come to Joseph to buy grain, to keep their families alive.

In Canaan, Jacob and his sons were hungry, too. When they heard there was food in Egypt, Jacob said to his sons, 'Go down to Egypt today – leave this minute! – and buy some grain for us. Otherwise we will die!' Then he clutched Simeon's arm. 'But don't take Benjamin with you. After losing Joseph, I couldn't bear it if anything happened to my young one.'

The ten brothers left for Egypt that day.

Now, as governor of the land of Egypt, Joseph knew every single thing that happened there. When a bird pecked at his corn, he could feel it. So when his brothers entered Egypt he heard at once, and sent for them.

He waited in his large elegant room, trembling. As soon as they entered the house, Joseph recognised his brothers. But he made no sign of it, even though his heart was pounding.

The brothers did not recognise Joseph. His hair was cut in the style of the Egyptians, his arms dazzling with bangles. They bowed down to the governor of the land with their faces to the ground.

Joseph turned away, tears filling his eyes. Seeing them bent before him, he remembered his dream of years ago. Here were the sheaves and stars, his brothers. Except in the dream there had been eleven of each.
Oh Lord, where was Benjamin?

Could he trust them? Joseph questioned his brothers about their family. They told him there was a younger brother waiting at home, and a poor old hungry father. Joseph longed to see Benjamin, so he called the guards to take Simeon – saying that he would release him only when his brothers returned with Benjamin.

'I believe you are spies,' he told them. 'You must prove to me that you are telling the truth. Let me see this youngest brother that you speak of, or you will all be thrown into prison.'

The brothers threw up their hands in horror. 'Oh no,' they pleaded, 'what will our poor dear father say?' And amongst themselves, they whispered and wept.

'Surely we are being punished because of our brother Joseph,' murmured Judah. 'I remember how he pleaded with us for his life, and we just ignored him!'

'Didn't I *tell* you not to sin against the boy?' Reuben hissed. 'But you wouldn't listen . . .'

Joseph turned away. The brothers thought he couldn't understand their language, but as Joseph listened a terrible sadness and anger and love wrestled in his chest, like lions in a cage. Let me out, he wanted to say. See who I am? It's me, Joseph – your brother!

As he looked at his brothers, he remembered the boy he once was – how he ran about the fields, his father's love warm on his skin like the sun. He thought of his childhood lost forever, and the memories burnt his lungs and throat so that he could hardly speak. But still he didn't share his secret...

So the brothers went home with their grain and a promise to Joseph to bring back their little brother. When the grain was gone and not a crumb of food remained, old Jacob wept, waving goodbye to Benjamin.

When Joseph saw his little brother, tears rose up in his eyes. He rubbed at them, and ordered food and wine for a banquet. After he'd filled Benjamin's plate five times over, with goose and pomegranates and figs and five kinds of bread, he tested his older brothers still further. But when they were on their knees, begging for his mercy, Joseph could no longer hold his secret in.

'Look!' he cried. 'Don't you know who I am? I'm Joseph – the brother you sold into Egypt!'

The brothers moaned with terror, but Joseph held out his hands to them. 'Come close to me, don't be afraid.'

When Joseph stood surrounded by his brothers, feeling their warmth in the cool silent room, he saw all the dreams he'd had, laid out like beautiful paintings, one next to the other. He saw they were signposts painted by God, and he could only have followed them, as his brothers had.

'Don't be angry with yourselves,' he said. 'The day you sent me to Egypt, you saved all our lives. See? I'm now ruler of all the land. It was God who sent me ahead to help our family survive. Now go and tell our father the news, and bring him here. There are five more years of famine, and I'll make sure we and all our children will live well and happily here on this soil.'

And so it was that Jacob travelled to Egypt and saw his son Joseph once again, his blessed child with the quick smile and shining eyes, the master of dreams.